great
ground meat
recipes

TRIDENT
PRESS
INTERNATIONAL

Published by:
TRIDENT PRESS INTERNATIONAL
801 12th Avenue South
Suite 302
Naples, FL 34102 U.S.A.
Copyright(c)Trident Press International
Tel: (941) 649 7077
Fax: (941) 649 5832
Email: tridentpress@worldnet.att.net
Website: www.trident-international.com

acknowledgements

Great Ground Meat Recipes

Compiled by: R&R Publications Marketing P/L
Creative Director: Paul Sims
Production Manager: Anthony Carroll
Food Photography: Warren Webb,
Andrew Elton, Quentin Bacon, Per Ericson,
Paul Grater, Ray Joice, John Stewart,
Ashley Mackevicius, Harm Mol,
Yanto Noerianto, Andy Payne.
Food Stylists: Wendy Berecry,
Michelle Gorry, Donna Hay.
Recipe Development: Ellen Argyriou,
Sheryle Eastwood, Lucy Kelly, Donna Hay,
Anneka Mitchell, Penelope Peel,
Jody Vassallo,Loukie Werle.
Proof Reader: Samantha Calcott

Includes Index
ISBN 1582790612
EAN 9781582790619

First Edition Printed June 2001
Computer Typeset in Humanist 521
& Times New Roman

Printed in Hong Kong

contents

Introduction
4

Points for success
6

Ground beef
8

Ground chicken
32

Ground lamb
50

Ground pork
62

Weights and measures
78

Index
80

introduction

introduction

The wonderful recipes and ideas in this book for preparing and serving ground meat are sure to impress family and friends. Ground meat is a popular, economic and without doubt the most versatile form of meat. Just think of what you can do with it – roll or shape it, then poach, bake, pan cook, stir-fry or even roast it. Supermarkets and butchers, recognising the popularity of ground meat, plus the fact that many people are becoming increasing health-conscious, are now producing low-fat or slimmer's ground meat. This is a boom for the family slimmer and those who are generally concerned about what they and their families are eating. The recipes in this book use lean ground meat, however they are just as delicious made with standard ground meat.

Nutritive value of meat

Lean ground beef, chicken, lamb and pork are highly nutritious foods with unique features. Packed full of high quality protein and essential vitamins and minerals, meat is a valuable contributor to a healthy body.

One of meat's prime nutritional benefits is as a supplier of the mineral iron. Iron is indispensable to carrying oxygen around our bodies, via our bloodstream. If you do not eat enough iron, you may become tired, have poor stamina and even become anaemic.

Lean ground beef, chicken, lamb and pork are some of the highest iron foods and this so called "haem iron" is the most easily used by our bodies. The haem iron in meat also helps the body maximise the iron in poorer iron ("non haem") foods such as vegetables, nuts, legumes and grains.

An average serve of lean red meat not only boosts your iron status, it easily provides up to half your daily requirements of zinc. Zinc is another mineral essential for humans, being necessary for growth and reproduction, healing and a healthy immune system.

That serving of meat is also brimming with B vitamins. Valuable thiamin, riboflavin, niacin, vitamin B6 and vitamin B12 will all be supplied in significant quantities, helping to release energy from food and maintain a healthy body. High quality protein, essential for the building and repair of all body cells will also be provided. Meat protein is perfectly matched to your body's needs, as it contains all of the 8 essential amino acids, or protein "building blocks', needed each day.

Lean ground beef, chicken, lamb and pork are a unique combination of many essential nutrients in the one versatile, low fat package. They make a great tasting and nutritious contribution to any meal.

Purchasing of meat

Getting the best out of your meat buying relies on the correct choice, the correct purchasing and storage of the meat, and the correct cooking method for the meat selected.

- Only buy the amount of meat that can be stored correctly in the space available.
- Before setting out to purchase a fresh supply of meat, prepare the refrigerator and freezer to store the meat. Make the necessary space available, wash meat trays and defrost the refrigerator and freezer if necessary, so that the meat will be stored immediately on arriving home.
- Choose meat which is bright pink to red in colour with a fresh (not dry) appearance.
- Keep meat cold while carrying home to prevent the growth of food spoilage bacteria. This may be achieved by using an insulated chiller bag.
  For larger quantities, if transporting by car, place an Eskie with a cooling brick in the car and store the meat in it immediately it is purchased, particularly if departure for home is not immediate.
- If you are unsure about which cuts of meat to buy ask advice from your local butcher. Butchers are trained professionals with a wealth of useful information and are always willing to assist.

- If calculating the quantity of meat to buy for a meal is a problem, allow 125g/4oz to 150g/5oz of lean boneless meat per person.

Storage of meat

In the Meat Compartment:
- Remove from pre-package (plastic makes meat sweat which shortens storage life) and arrange in stacks no more than 2-3 layers high. Make sure there is some air space between each piece of meat. Cover top of meat loosely with foil to stop surface drying.

In the Refrigerator Cabinet:
- Place a stainless steel or plastic rack in a dish deep enough to catch any meat drip. Unwrap meat and store as for "Meat Compartment" in coldest part of refrigerator. In a "refrigerator only" unit this is at the bottom. In a combination refrigerator freezer, the coldest air is at the top of the refrigerator, because of closeness to freezer.
- If meat is to be used on day of purchase, it can be left in its original wrapping.
- Meat kept in the refrigerator for 2-3 days will be more tender than meat cooked on day of purchase. This is because natural enzymes soften the meat fibres.
- Ground meat and sausages refrigerate for 2 days

Freezer storage of meat
- Trim visible fat off meat completely or leave a small selvedge.
- Pack ground meat in meal size portions in a freezer storage bag. Press out as flat as possible, seal and label. Wide, thin packages will thaw quicker than narrow, thick packages.
- Use freezer storage bags, or plastic wrap. Wrap well to exclude air and prevent freezer burn. When placing in the freezer bag, press out as much air as possible then fold over and tape end down.

- Lable packages with name, the amount and date of freezing.
- Leave sausages in links and place meal size portions in freezer bags, seal and label.
- Rotate stocks - first in first out.
- Defrost meats in the refrigerator, never at room temperature or in water. Allow 2 days for a large roast, 1 day or less for smaller cuts, according to quantity. Do not remove from package when thawing. Meat may also be defrosted quickly in a microwave oven. Follow manufacturer's instructions.
- Do not refreeze thawed meat unless cooked first.
- Do not overstock freezer, as its effectiveness will diminish. Frozen meats must be stored at a constant temperature of - 15°C/0°F.
- Prolonged storage time in the freezer will result in loss of quality. The following guide will assist.
- Ground meat and sausages freeze for 2-3 months

points for
success

Cooking ground meat

Ground meat meat has many cut surfaces and therefore more vulnerable to spoilage by microorganisms than any other meat. Extra care must be taken during transport home and storage. Transport home quickly, make meat the last item on your shopping list, or take an insulated bag to place it in.

To freeze ground meat place it in plastic freezer bags about 500g/1lb per bag. Press out flat into corners, expel air and tape down. Label and date, use within 2 months. Flat pack ground meat defrosts more quickly than a thick ball of ground meat. If all of the pack is not to be used, a thin pack can easily be cut in half, before thawing. Do not refreeze ground meat that has been thawed. If using ground chicken to make loaves, rissoles and patties you will need the addition of breadcrumbs to lighten the texture. About 1/2 cup of dried or fresh breadcrumbs to 500g/1lb of ground meat. More may be added if you wish to extend the ground meat. Moisture is also required, a little oil or water will suffice, and a whole egg added or just the egg white will bind the mixture.

Flavour is added with salt, pepper, fresh chopped onion and a little garlic. Other flavours may be achieved by adding curry powder or chopped dried fruits.

Remember to mix well, kneading by hand is the best method. To shape balls or rissoles, wet hands first so that the ground meat does not stick to the hands.

Cooking sausages

- When grilling, roasting, barbecuing or frying sausages, it is usual to prick the skins to prevent them from bursting.
- An alternative method is to moisten them with warm water first to make their skins stretch, which will prevent them from bursting.
- Always cook sausages over moderate heat, so that heat can penetrate to centre. Quick cooking over high heat will scorch the outside and leave the centre raw. They will also burst their skins even though they have been pricked.
- Grilled, barbecued and roasted thick sausages take 15 minutes to cook and need turning often. Fried sausages take 12 minutes. Thin sausages take 2 minutes less.
- Blanching sausages before grilling, barbecuing or frying prevents them bursting, removes some of the fat and makes them quicker to cook. This method is ideal when cooking large quantities for a gathering. Place them in hot water, bring them to a simmer and simmer for 5 minutes. Remove and dry on paper towels. Proceed to cook on grill or barbecue.

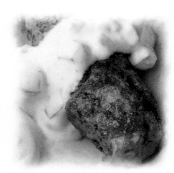

Photograph page 7 also appears on recipe page 28 (Meatball and Bean Salad)

*carpetburgers with caper
mayonnaise*

ground
beef

If   a recipe requires ground meat,

to be browned, heat a little oil in a saucepan, add
ground meat and stir continuously until ground
meat changes from red to a light brown colour.
Ground meat must all break up and not form into
lumps. Break up lumps as they form with the back of
spoon or fork. For diet cooking and particularly when
using very low fat ground meat, just place the ground
meat in a saucepan and add water to make it very
moist. Place on the heat and stir until ground meat
changes from pink to grey. Add flavourings and simmer.
Ground meat needs to simmer for 25-30 minutes.

carpetburgers
with caper mayonnaise

Photograph page 9

ingredients

500g/1 lb lean ground beef
250g/8oz sausage meat
4 spring onions, finely chopped
2 cloves garlic, crushed
2 teaspoons finely grated lemon rind
1 teaspoon finely chopped fresh dill
18 bottled oysters
3 rashers bacon, cut in half lengthwise
and rind removed
2 tablespoons red wine
2 tablespoons olive oil

Caper mayonnaise
2 tablespoons mayonnaise
1/2 cup/125mL/4fl oz cream (double)
2 teaspoons chopped capers
1 teaspoon finely grated lemon rind
1 small gherkin, finely chopped

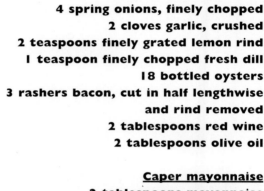

Method:

1 Place beef, sausage meat, spring onions, garlic, lemon rind and dill in a bowl and mix to combine. Shape mixture into twelve patties.

2 Top half the patties with 3 oysters each, then, with remaining patties, inch edges together to join and completely seal the filling. Wrap a piece of bacon around each pattie and secure with wooden toothpicks or cocktail sticks.

3 Place wine and oil in a large shallow glass or ceramic dish and mix to combine. Add patties and marinate for 10 minutes.

4 Drain patties and cook on a preheated medium barbecue for 5-7 minutes each side or until cooked.

5 To make mayonnaise, place mayonnaise, cream, capers, lemon rind and gherkin in a bowl and mix to combine. Serve with patties.

Note: A more economical, but just as tasty variation on that old favourite Carpetbag Steak. Prunes, dried apricots or sliced cheese can be used in place of the oysters.

Serves 6

chilli
con carne

Method:

1 Heat olive oil in a frying pan over a medium heat, add onion, garlic and green pepper and cook, stirring, for 3-4 minutes or until onion is soft. Stir in beef and cook for 5 minutes or until meat is brown.

2 Add paprika, chilli powder, cumin, chilli, tomato purée (passata), stock and wine to meat mixture, bring to simmering and simmer, stirring occasionally, for 25 minutes or until liquid is reduced by half. Stir in beans and black pepper to taste and cook for 10 minutes longer.

3 Heat vegetable oil in a large saucepan until a cube of bread dropped in browns in 50 seconds. Cook tortillas one at a time, pushing down with a small ladle, to make a basket shape, for 3-4 minutes or until golden. Drain on absorbent kitchen paper. Spoon meat mixture into tortilla baskets and top with sour cream.

Note: Another easy serving idea for this spicy meat mixture is to spoon it over hot baked potatoes. Cook four large potatoes in the oven at 200°C/400°F/Gas 6 for 1 hour or the microwave on HIGH (100%) for 15 minutes or until tender. Cut a cross in the top of the potatoes and using a clean cloth push up. Spoon meat mixture over potatoes and top with sour cream.

Serves 4

ingredients

1 tablespoon olive oil
1 onion, finely chopped
2 cloves garlic, crushed
1 green pepper, chopped
500g/1 lb lean ground beef
2 teaspoons ground paprika
$^1/_2$ teaspoon chilli powder
$^1/_2$ teaspoon ground cumin
1 teaspoon ground red chilli
440g/14oz canned tomato
purée (passata)
$^1/_2$ cup/125mL/4fl oz beef stock
$^1/_2$ cup/125mL/4fl oz red wine
315g/10oz canned red kidney beans,
drained and rinsed
freshly ground black pepper
vegetable oil for deep-frying
4 tortillas
$^1/_2$ cup/125g/4oz sour cream

Oven temperature 200°C, 400°F, Gas 6

nasi goreng

Photograph page 13

Method:

1 To make meatballs, place beef, onion, chilli, curry paste (vindaloo) and egg white in a bowl and mix to combine. Shape meat mixture into small balls.

2 Heat vegetable oil in a large saucepan until a cube of bread dropped in browns in 50 seconds. Cook meatballs a few at a time for 4-5 minutes or until golden and cooked through. Drain meatballs on absorbent kitchen paper, then thread onto short bamboo skewers, set aside and keep warm.

3 For rice, place eggs and 1 teaspoon soy sauce in a bowl and whisk to combine. Heat 1 tablespoon peanut (groundnut) oil in a heavy-based frying pan over a medium heat, add egg mixture and cook, without stirring, until set. Remove omelette from pan, cut half into small pieces and half into long strips. Set aside.

4 Heat remaining peanut (groundnut) oil in frying pan over a medium heat, add onions, garlic, red and green capsicums (peppers) and stir-fry for 3-4 minutes or until onion is soft. Add chilli, chicken and pork and stir-fry for 8-10 minutes longer or until meat is brown.

5 Add prawns (shrimp), bean sprouts and rice and stir-fry for 4-5 minutes or until mixture is heated through. Stir in coriander, chopped omelette and remaining soy sauce and stir-fry for 1-2 minutes longer.

6 To serve, spoon rice into the centre of a serving platter, top with omelette strips and surround with skewered meatballs.

Note: In this version of a traditional Indonesian dish ground chicken or pork are delicious alternatives for the meatballs.

Serves 6

ingredients

Chilli meatballs
250g/8oz lean ground beef
1 onion, finely chopped
1/2 teaspoon ground red chilli
1/2 teaspoon curry paste (vindaloo)
1 egg white, lightly beaten
vegetable oil for deep-frying

Nasi goreng rice
2 eggs, lightly beaten
1 tablespoon soy sauce
1/4 cup/60mL/2fl oz peanut
(groundnut) oil
2 onions, thinly sliced
2 cloves garlic, crushed
1/2 red capsicum (pepper), chopped
1/2 green capsicum (pepper), chopped
1 teaspoon ground red chilli
1 boneless chicken breast fillet, chopped
1 x 375g/12oz fillet pork, chopped
250g/8oz uncooked prawns (shrimp),
shelled and deveined
125g/4oz bean sprouts
2 1/4 cups/500g/1 lb long grain rice, cooked
1 tablespoon chopped fresh coriander

nasi goreng

sausage
and roasted capsicum (pepper) salad

Method:

1 *To make sausages, place beef, sausage meat, garlic, rosemary, basil, proscuitto or ham, olive oil and black pepper to taste in a bowl and mix to combine. Shape mixture into 10cm/4in long sausages. Cook sausages under a preheated medium grill, turning occasionally, for 10-15 minutes or until brown and cooked through. Set aside to cool slightly, then cut each sausage into diagonal slices.*

2 *To make dressing, place olive oil, vinegar, basil, oregano and black pepper to taste in a screwtop jar and shake well to combine.*

3 *Place sausage slices, penne, red capsicum (peppers), yellow or green capsicum (peppers), mushrooms and olives in bowl, spoon over dressing and toss to combine. Line a serving platter with spinach leaves, then top with sausage and vegetable mixture.*

Note: *To prevent pasta that is for use in a salad from sticking together, rinse it under cold running water immediately after draining. All this mouth-watering salad needs to make a complete meal is some crusty bread or wholemeal rolls.*

Serves 4

sausage and roasted capsicum (pepper) salad

ingredients

125g/4oz penne, cooked and cooled
2 red capsicum (peppers),
roasted and cut into strips
2 yellow or green capsicum (peppers),
roasted and cut into strips
125g/4oz button mushrooms, sliced
155g/5oz pitted black olives
5 English spinach leaves, stalks
removed and leaves finely chopped

Herbed beef sausages
500g/1 lb lean ground beef
185g/6oz sausage meat
2 cloves garlic, crushed
1 teaspoon chopped fresh rosemary
1 tablespoon finely chopped fresh basil
2 slices proscuitto or lean ham,
finely chopped
1 tablespoon olive oil
freshly ground black pepper

Herb dressing
1/2 cup/125mL/4fl oz olive oil
1/4 cup/60mL/2fl oz balsamic or
red wine vinegar
2 teaspoons chopped fresh basil or
1 teaspoon dried basil
1 teaspoon chopped fresh oregano or
1/2 teaspoon dried oregano
freshly ground black pepper

middle
eastern meatballs

Method:

1 Place beef, couscous, allspice, parsley and egg in a bowl and mix to combine. Shape into small balls, coat with flour and set aside.

2 Heat ghee or butter in a large saucepan and cook meatballs in batches, for 5 minutes or until brown on all sides. Return meatballs to pan, pour in stock, add cinnamon stick and bring to boil. Reduce heat and simmer for 10 minutes.

3 Stir honey, saffron, nutmeg, sultanas, apricots and chutney into pan, cover and simmer for 30 minutes. Stir in orange juice and simmer, uncovered, for 10 minutes longer or until liquid reduces and thickens slightly. Serve sprinkled with orange rind and almonds.

Note: These meatballs look great served on a bed of saffron rice or couscous. To make saffron rice, soak a few strands of saffron in 3 tablespoons warm water and add to water when cooking the rice. Instead of saffron you can use $^1/_4$ teaspoon ground turmeric, in which case there is no need to soak it; simply add to the water and rice.

Serves 4

ingredients

500g/1 lb lean ground beef
60g/2oz couscous, cooked
1 teaspoon ground allspice
2 tablespoons chopped fresh parsley
1 egg, lightly beaten
flour
60g/2oz ghee or butter
2 cups/500mL/16fl oz beef stock
1 cinnamon stick
2 tablespoons honey
$^1/_4$ teaspoon saffron powder
$^1/_2$ teaspoon ground nutmeg
3 tablespoons sultanas
3 tablespoons chopped dried apricots
2 tablespoons fruit chutney
$^1/_4$ cup/60mL/2fl oz orange juice
2 teaspoons grated orange rind
30g/1oz blanched almonds, toasted

crunchy
cottage pie

Method:

1 Heat oil in a frying pan over a medium heat, add onion and cook, stirring, for 1 minute. Add garlic, mushrooms and bacon and cook, stirring constantly, for 2 minutes. Stir in beef and cook for 5 minutes or until meat is brown.

2 Stir tomato sauce, Worcestershire sauce, soy sauce, stock, thyme, parsley and black pepper to taste into pan. Bring to simmering and simmer, uncovered, for 25-30 minutes or until mixture reduces and thickens. Spoon meat mixture into an ovenproof pie dish.

3 To make topping, place potatoes, pumpkin or carrots, egg, sour cream and nutmeg in a bowl and mix to combine. Spoon vegetable mixture over meat mixture. Place pumpkin seeds (pepitas), breadcrumbs, Parmesan cheese and butter in a bowl and mix to combine. Sprinkle over vegetable mixture and bake for 45 minutes or until meat mixture is hot and bubbling and topping is golden.

Note: Any ground meat or combination of ground meats can be used to make this tasty cottage pie. The pie is almost a meal in itself, all you need for a complete meal are steamed green vegetables such as zucchini (courgettes), beans or cabbage.

Serves 4

ingredients

1 tablespoon olive oil
1 onion, finely chopped
1 clove garlic, crushed
125g/4oz mushrooms, sliced
2 rashers bacon, chopped
500g/1 lb lean ground beef
3 tablespoons tomato sauce
1½ tablespoons Worcestershire sauce
1 teaspoon soy sauce
1¾ cup/440mL/14fl oz beef stock
¼ teaspoon dried thyme
2 tablespoons chopped fresh parsley
freshly ground black pepper

Crunchy vegetable topping
3 large potatoes, chopped
250g/8oz pumpkin or carrots, chopped
1 egg, lightly beaten
¼ cup/60g/2oz sour cream
¼ teaspoon nutmeg
¼ cup/30g/1oz chopped pumpkin seeds
(pepitas)
¼ cup/30g/1oz dried breadcrumbs
30g/1oz grated fresh Parmesan cheese
60g/2oz butter, melted

Oven temperature 180°C/350°F/Gas 4

crunchy cottage pie

devilled
corn muffins

Method:

1 *To make filling, heat oil in a frying pan over a medium heat, add beef and cook, stirring, for 5 minutes or until meat is brown. Stir in curry powder and brown sugar and cook for 2 minutes longer. Mix in tomato sauce, Worcestershire sauce, soy sauce and lemon juice and bring to the boil. Reduce heat and simmer for 10 minutes or until mixture thickens. Set aside to cool.*

2 *Place flour, corn meal (polenta), sugar, cayenne pepper, pimiento or red capsicum (pepper) and cheese in a bowl and mix to combine. Stir in butter, milk and eggs and mix until just combined.*

3 *Half fill lightly greased muffin tins with corn meal (polenta) mixture, then top with a heaped teaspoonful of filling and enough corn meal (polenta) mixture to almost fill the tins. Bake for 20-25 minutes or until muffins are cooked when tested with a skewer.*

Makes 12

ingredients

2 cups/250g/8oz self-raising flour, sifted
²/₃ cup/125g/4oz corn meal (polenta)
2 tablespoons sugar
pinch cayenne pepper
3 tablespoons chopped bottled pimiento
or roasted red capsicum (pepper)
90g/3oz tasty cheese
(mature cheddar), grated
125g/4oz butter, melted
³/₄ cup/185mL/6fl oz milk
2 eggs, lightly beaten

<u>Devilled beef filling</u>
1 tablespoon vegetable oil
250g/8oz lean ground beef
1 teaspoon curry powder
2 tablespoons brown sugar
2 tablespoons tomato sauce
2 teaspoons Worcestershire sauce
1 teaspoon soy sauce
2 teaspoons lemon juice

Oven temperature 200°C, 400°F, Gas 6

crispy
chilli turnovers

Method:

1 To make filling, melt ghee or butter in a large frying pan over a medium heat, add beef and cook, stirring, for 5 minutes. Stir in onion, ginger, garlic, chilli, turmeric, cumin, garam masala and black pepper to taste and cook until onion is soft.

2 Stir stock and chutney into meat mixture and bring to the boil. Reduce heat and simmer for 20 minutes or until most of the liquid evaporates. Remove pan from heat and set aside to cool.

3 Roll out pastry on a lightly floured surface to 5mm/¹/₄in thick and using a 7¹/₂cm/3in cutter cut out rounds.

4 Place a spoonful of the meat mixture in the centre of each pastry round. Brush edges lightly with water and fold pastry over filling. Press edges together, then pinch with your thumb and index finger. Fold pinched edges over and pinch again.

5 Heat oil in a large saucepan until a cube of bread dropped in browns in 50 seconds and cook a few turnovers at a time for 3-4 minutes or until filling is cooked and pastry golden.

Serves 6

ingredients

500g/1 lb prepared puff pastry
vegetable oil for deep-frying

Spicy beef filling
30g/1oz ghee or butter
500g/1 lb lean ground beef
1 onion, finely chopped
2 teaspoons finely grated fresh ginger
2 cloves garlic, crushed
1 small fresh green or red chilli, finely chopped
¹/₂ teaspoon ground turmeric
¹/₂ teaspoon ground cumin
¹/₂ teaspoon garam masala
freshly ground black pepper
¹/₂ cup/125mL/4fl oz beef stock
1 tablespoon lime or mango chutney

burritos
with avocado mayonnaise

Photograph page 21

ingredients

1 tablespoon vegetable oil
1 onion, finely chopped
500g/1 lb lean ground beef
30g/1oz packet chilli seasoning mix
1/2 cup/125mL/4fl oz bottled tomato salsa
440g/14oz canned tomatoes, undrained and mashed
1/2 cup/125mL/4fl oz beef stock
315g/10oz canned red kidney beans, drained and rinsed
8 tortillas
90g/3oz butter, melted
1 red capsicum (pepper), cut into strips

<u>Avocado mayonnaise</u>
1 large avocado, peeled and seeded
1/2 cup/125g/4oz sour cream
1/4 cup/60mL/2fl oz thickened (double) cream
2 teaspoons lemon juice
1 tablespoon mayonnaise
pinch chilli powder

Oven temperature 150°C, 300°F, Gas 2

Method:

1 *Heat oil in a frying pan over a medium heat, add onion and cook for 3-4 minutes or until soft. Add beef and cook, stirring, until meat is brown. Stir in seasoning mix, salsa, tomatoes, stock and beans and bring to the boil. Reduce heat and simmer for 20 minutes or until mixture thickens slightly. Remove pan from heat and set aside to cool.*

2 *Brush tortillas with butter and stack on a greased 30x60cm/12x24in piece of aluminium foil. Wrap tortillas tightly in foil and bake for 15 minutes.*

3 *Spoon meat mixture into the centre of each tortilla. Fold tortilla like an envelope to form a parcel and place seam side down in a shallow ovenproof dish. Brush with butter and bake at 180°C/350°F/Gas 4 for 15 minutes or until heated through.*

4 *To make mayonnaise, place avocado, sour cream, cream, lemon juice, mayonnaise and chilli powder in a food processor or blender and process until smooth.*

5 *To serve, spoon mayonnaise over hot burritos and top with red capsicum (pepper) strips.*

Serves 8

new spaghetti
and meatballs

new spaghetti and meatballs

ingredients

500g/1 lb lean ground beef
1 onion, finely chopped
1 clove garlic, crushed
1 tablespoon finely chopped fresh basil
or 1 teaspoon dried basil
4 slices Italian salami, finely chopped
2 teaspoons tomato paste (purée)
1 egg, lightly beaten
flour
2 tablespoons olive oil
250g/8oz spaghetti
60g/2oz grated fresh Parmesan cheese

<u>Sun-dried tomato sauce</u>
30g/1oz butter
1 clove garlic, crushed
4 slices proscuitto or ham, chopped
2 tablespoons chopped fresh rosemary
or 1 teaspoon dried rosemary
1/2 cup/125mL/4fl oz chicken stock
1/2 cup/125mL/4fl oz red wine
16 sun-dried tomatoes in olive oil,
drained and chopped
freshly ground black pepper
2 tablespoons chopped fresh basil

Method:

1 *Place beef, onion, garlic, basil, salami, tomato paste (purée) and egg in a bowl and mix to combine. Shape mixture into small balls and roll in flour.*

2 *Heat oil in a large frying pan over a medium heat and cook meatballs in batches, for 5 minutes or until brown on all sides. Remove meatballs from pan and set aside.*

3 *To make sauce, wipe pan clean, add butter and melt over a medium heat. Add garlic, proscuitto or ham and rosemary and cook for 2 minutes. Stir in stock and wine and return meatballs to pan. Bring to the boil, then reduce heat and simmer for 15 minutes. Stir in sun-dried tomatoes and black pepper to taste and continue to cook until sauce reduces slightly. Remove pan from heat and stir in basil.*

4 *Cook pasta in boiling water in a large saucepan following packet directions. Drain well. To serve, spoon meatballs and sauce over hot spaghetti and sprinkle with Parmesan cheese.*

Note: *When shaping ground meat, dampen you hands and work on a lightly floured or dampened surface — this prevents the ground meat from sticking to your hands and the work surface. An egg added to ground meat mixtures binds them and makes them easier to shape.*

Serves 4

beefy egg pies

Method:

1. To make filling, heat oil in a frying pan over a medium heat, add onion and bacon and cook, stirring, for 3-4 minutes. Stir in beef and cook for 5 minutes or until meat is brown. Add flour and thyme and cook, stirring constantly, for 2 minutes. Stir in tomato sauce, Worcestershire sauce, stock, cornflour mixture and black pepper to taste and bring to the boil. Reduce heat and simmer for 5 minutes or until mixture thickens. Remove pan from heat and set aside to cool.

2. Line base and sides of eight greased small metal pie dishes with shortcrust pastry. Divide filling between pie dishes. Using the back of a spoon, make a depression in the centre of filling mixture and carefully slide an egg into each hollow. Sprinkle with cheese.

3. Cut rounds of puff pastry to fit tops of pies. Brush edges of shortcrust pastry with water, then top with puff pastry. Press edges together to seal. Brush with egg mixture, make two slits in the top of each pie and bake for 20-25 minutes or until golden.

Note: When you are making a pie with a cooked filling it is important that the filling is cold before you place it in the pie dish and top with the pastry lid. If the filling is hot or warm it will cause the pastry to go tough and soggy.

Makes 8

ingredients

750g/1 1/2 lb prepared shortcrust pastry
375g/12oz prepared puff pastry
1 egg, lightly beaten with
1 tablespoon water

Beef filling
1 tablespoon vegetable oil
1 onion, chopped
2 rashers bacon, chopped
375g/12oz lean ground beef
1 tablespoon flour
1/2 teaspoon dried thyme
1/4 cup/60mL/2fl oz tomato sauce
1 tablespoon Worcestershire sauce
1 cup/250mL/8fl oz beef stock
2 teaspoons cornflour blended with
1 tablespoon water
freshly ground black pepper
8 eggs
125g/4oz grated tasty cheese
(mature cheddar)

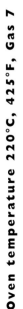

Oven temperature 220°C, 425°F, Gas 7

23

Method:

1 *Place beef, sausage meat, coriander, garlic, cumin and black pepper to taste in bowl and mix to combine. Set aside.*

2 *Toss hard-boiled eggs in flour. Divide meat mixture into eight portions. Using floured hands mould one portion of meat around each egg.*

3 *Place beaten egg and milk in a shallow dish and whisk to combine. Place breadcrumbs and sesame seeds in a separate shallow dish and mix to combine. Dip meat-coated eggs in egg mixture, then roll in breadcrumb mixture to coat. Place on a plate lined with plastic food wrap and refrigerate for 30 minutes.*

4 *Heat vegetable oil in a large saucepan until a cube of bread dropped in browns in 50 seconds. Cook prepared eggs a few at a time for 7-10 minutes or until golden and cooked through. Drain on absorbent kitchen paper and keep warm.*

5 *To make sauce, heat peanut (groundnut) oil in a saucepan over a medium heat, add onion, garlic and ginger and cook, stirring, for 2-3 minutes or until onion is soft. Stir in coconut milk, lime juice, peanut butter and chilli powder and cook, stirring constantly, until heated and well blended.*
Serve with Spicy Egg Balls.

Note: *This recipe is a variation on the old favourite Scotch Eggs. For something different use ground pork instead of beef. Just as good cold, these Spicy Egg Balls are great picnic food and leftovers are popular for packed lunches.*

Serves 4

spicy
egg balls

Photograph page 25

ingredients

250g/8oz lean ground beef
250g/8oz sausage meat
**2 tablespoons finely chopped
fresh coriander**
2 cloves garlic, crushed
I teaspoon ground cumin
freshly ground black pepper
8 hard-boiled eggs
flour
I egg, lightly beaten
2 tablespoons milk
2 cups/250g/8oz dried breadcrumbs
2 tablespoons sesame seeds
vegetable oil for deep-frying

Peanut sauce
I tablespoon peanut (groundnut) oil
I small onion, finely chopped
I clove garlic, crushed
1/2 teaspoon finely grated fresh ginger
I cup/250mL/8fl oz coconut milk
I tablespoon lime juice
4 tablespoons crunchy peanut butter
pinch of chilli powder

wellington
bread loaf

Photograph page 27

Method:

1 *Cut base from bread loaf and reserve. Scoop bread from centre of loaf leaving a 1cm/¹/₂in shell. Make bread from centre into crumbs and set aside. Brush inside of bread shell with butter, spread with pâté, then press mushroom slices into pâté.*

2 *Place 1 cup/60g/2oz reserved breadcrumbs (keep remaining breadcrumbs for another use), beef, chives, black peppercorns, eggs, stock cube and tomato paste (purée) in a bowl and mix to combine.*

3 *Spoon beef mixture into bread shell, packing down well. Reposition base and wrap loaf in aluminium foil. Place loaf on a baking tray and bake for 1¹/₂ hours or until meat mixture is cooked.*

4 *To make sauce, melt butter in a saucepan over a medium heat, stir in flour and cook, stirring, for 1 minute. Remove pan from heat and gradually whisk in stock and wine. Return pan to heat and cook, stirring constantly, for 4-5 minutes or until sauce boils and thickens. Serve sauce with meatloaf.*

Note: *Breadcrumbs are easy to make, simply place the bread in a food processor and process to make crumbs, if you do not have a food processor rub the bread through a sieve. Breadcrumbs should be made with stale bread; for this recipe either use a loaf of bread that is a day or two old or scoop out the centre of the loaf as described in the recipe, then spread the bread out on a tray and leave for 2-3 hours to become stale, before making into crumbs.*

Serves 8

ingredients

1 Vienna bread loaf
30g/1oz butter, melted
250g/8oz liver pâté
125g/4oz button mushrooms, sliced
750g/1¹/₂ lb lean ground beef
2 tablespoons snipped fresh chives
2 teaspoons crushed black peppercorns
2 eggs, lightly beaten
¹/₂ beef stock cube
1 tablespoon tomato paste (purée)

Red wine and thyme sauce
30g/1oz butter
2 tablespoons flour
¹/₂ cup/125mL/4fl oz beef stock
¹/₂ cup/125mL/4fl oz dry red wine
freshly ground black pepper

Oven temperature 180°C, 350°F, Gas 4

meatball
and bean salad

Photograph page 7 and below

Method:

1 Place onion, garlic, chilli powder, cumin, beef, tomato paste (purée), cheese, bread and egg white in a food processor and process to combine. Shape mixture into small balls.

2 Heat oil in a nonstick frying pan over a medium heat and cook meatballs in batches for 4-5 minutes or until brown and cooked through. Drain on absorbent kitchen paper.

3 To make dressing, place oil, vinegar, salsa, sugar, chilli and parsley in a screwtop jar and shake well to combine.

4 Place meatballs, beans and tomatoes in a large salad bowl. Spoon over dressing and toss to combine.

Note: Canola oil is the oil extracted from the rape plant, a member of the cabbage family. It differs from traditional rapeseed oil in that it does not contain the high levels of erucic acid. This has made rape a vaulable crop, as consumption of large quantities of eruric acid by humans has been shown to cause changes to heart muscles.

Serves 4

ingredients

**1 onion, chopped
1 clove garlic, crushed
1/2 teaspoon chilli powder
2 teaspoons ground cumin
500g/1 lb lean beef mince
2 tablespoons tomato paste (purée)
60g/2oz tasty cheese
(mature Cheddar), grated
1 slice white bread, crusts removed
1 egg white, lightly beaten
1 tablespoon canola or olive oil
2x440g/14oz canned three bean mix,
drain and rinsed
250g/8oz yellow teardrop or
cherry tomatoes**

**<u>Chilli dressing</u>
1/4 cup/60mL/2fl oz vegetable oil
1 1/2 tablespoons red wine vinegar
1/4 cup/60mL/2fl oz bottled tomato salsa
1/2 teaspoon sugar
1/2 teaspoon bottled minced chilli
2 tablespoons chopped fresh parsley**

classic
lasagne

Method:

1 Meat Sauce: *Brown beef in hot oil. Add remaining ingredients, cover and simmer for 20 minutes, stirring occasionally during cooking. Remove bay leaf.*

2 Cheese Sauce: *Melt butter, add flour and cook 1-2 minutes. Remove from heat, stir in milk and cheese. Bring to the boil stirring continuously. Season with salt, pepper and nutmeg.*

3 To Assemble:

a) *Spread 1/3 of the meat sauce over the base of a 20x30cm/8x12in ovenproof dish. Place a layer of lasagne pasta onto sauce.*

b) *Spread pasta with remaining meat sauce.*

c) *Top with another layer of lasagna sheets and spread with half the cheese sauce, sprinkle with mozzarella and parmesan cheese. Bake in a pre-heated oven at 190°C/370°F/Gas 5 for 30 minutes.*

d) *When cooked allow to stand for 5 minutes before cutting into squares to serve.*

Serves 4

ingredients

Meat Sauce
1 tablespoon olive oil
500g/1lb ground beef
1 onion, chopped
440g/14oz can peeled tomatoes
250g/8oz tomato paste
1 beef stock cube
1 teaspoon dried basil
1 teaspoon dried oregano
1 bay leaf
1/2 cup red wine

Cheese Sauce
3 tablespoons butter
3 tablespoons plain flour
2 cups milk
1/2 cup tasty cheese, grated
salt and pepper to taste
pinch of nutmeg

To Assemble
1 quantity of meat sauce
1 quantity of cheese sauce
250g/8oz packet of lasagne pasta
1 cup Mozzarella cheese
3 tablespoons grated
Parmesan cheese

Oven temperature 190°C, 370°F, Gas 5

clapshot
pie

Photograph page 31

Method:

1 Heat the oil in a frying pan, then fry the onion, carrot and bacon for 10 minutes or until browned. Add the mince and fry for 10-15 minutes, breaking up any lumps with the back of a wooden spoon, until the meat has browned. Spoon off any excess fat, then stir in the stock, ketchup, Worcestershire sauce, thyme and seasoning. Simmer, partly covered, for 45 minutes, stirring occasionally, until thickened. Add a little water if the mixture becomes too dry.

2 Meanwhile, cook the potatoes and swede in boiling salted water for 15-20 minutes, until tender. Drain, then mash with 25g/1oz butter and the cream. Season with pepper and nutmeg.

3 Preheat the oven to 200°C/400°F/Gas Mark 6. Transfer the beef to a 1 1/2 litre/2 3/4 pint shallow ovenproof dish, then stir in the parsley. Smooth over the potato and swede mixture, then fluff up with a fork and dot with the remaining butter. Bake for 35-45 minutes, until browned. Garnish with parsley.

Note: Clapshot is the Scottish name for a mixture of mashed potato and swede, hence the name of this version of cottage pie.

Serves 6

ingredients

1 tbsp olive or sunflower oil
1 large onion, chopped
1 large carrot, finely chopped
50g/2oz bacon, chopped
750g/1lb 11oz beef steak mince
300ml/1/2pint beef stock
2 tbsp tomato ketchup
1 tbsp Worcestershire sauce
1 tsp chopped fresh thyme
Salt and black pepper
2 tbsp chopped fresh parsley, plus extra to garnish

For the topping
450g/1lb potatoes, chopped
450g/1lb swede, chopped
50g/2oz butter
142ml carton single cream
Freshly grated nutmeg

Oven temperature 200°C, 400°F, Gas 6

chicken apricot roulade

ground chicken

Ground chicken is a combination

of white and dark chicken meat in equal proportions, which gives it tenderness and flavour. It can be made into all your old favourites; chicken meatloaf, rissoles, patties, chicken balls, burgers, chicken lasagne and chicken bolognese sauce. It is free of fat and therefore suitable for diet cooking where red ground meat may be too fatty.

chicken
apricot roulade

Photograph page 33 and below

Method:

1 *In a large bowl mix all the ingredients for the chicken roulade together, knead well with hand. Set aside. Reserve 5 apricots for garnish, place remainder with water and sugar in small saucepan, cover and cook until apricots are soft. Uncover and allow most of the water to evaporate. Stir well to form a purée. Mix in remaining ingredients.*

2 *Place a 35cm/14in length of plastic wrap on work bench. Spread over the ground chicken mixture to form a rectangle approximately 28x23cm/11x9in. Spread the apricot filling over the ground mixture. Lift the plastic wrap in front of you, holding it towards the ends, and fold over the mixture 4cm. Pull the wrap towards the back, forming a roll as you pull. Place on greased oven slide. Press 5 apricots along top. Brush with glaze, place in a preheated oven 180°C/350°C/Gas 4 for 40 minutes, brushing with glaze every 10 minutes. Serve roulade hot with vegetable accompaniments, or cold with salad.*

Serves 8

ingredients

Filling
1kg/2 lb ground chicken
120g/4oz dried apricots, chopped
1 cup/60g/2oz soft breadcrumbs
³/₄ cup/6fl oz water
1 small clove garlic, crushed
1 teaspoon sugar
1 teaspoon salt
1 small onion, finely chopped
¹/₄ teaspoon pepper
1 stick celery, diced
2 tablespoons lemon juice
1 tablespoon water

Glaze
2 tablespoons chopped parsley
heat together
2 tablespoons apricot jam,
1 tablespoon water and
2 teaspoons Teriyaki sauce

Oven temperature 180°C, 350°F, Gas 4

Oven temperature 180°C, 350°F, Gas 4

chicken
cannelloni

Method:

1 Heat butter in a large pan, add onion and sauté 2 minutes, add ground chicken and bacon and stir until browned and cooked. Remove from heat. Add Parmesan cheese, salt and pepper to taste. Set aside. .

2 Melt the 160g/5oz butter in a saucepan, add flour and stir 1 minute. Remove from heat, gradually add milk, stirring well. Return to heat, stir until sauce thickens and boils. Remove from heat, stir in seasonings, cheese and eggs. Fill cannelloni tubes with chicken mixture. Grease a large oven dish. Mix pasta sauce and water together and spread half over base of dish. Place cannelloni tubes in two rows in the dish then pour over remaining pasta sauce. Pour over the bechamel sauce, spread evenly and sprinkle with a little grated Parmesan cheese. Dot with 2 teaspoons butter and bake in preheated oven 180°C/350°F/Gas 4 for 30 to 35 minutes until golden brown. Serve hot with a tossed salad.

Serves 6

ingredients

2 tablespoons olive oil or butter
³/₄ cup/90g/3oz flour
1 onion, finely chopped
4 cups/1lt milk
500g/1lb ground chicken
salt, pepper
3 tablespoons grated Parmesan cheese
¹/₈ teaspoon nutmeg
2 eggs, beaten
cannelloni tubes
1 cup/250ml/8oz tomato pasta sauce
160g/5oz butter
¹/₂ cup/125ml/4fl oz water

curried
chicken rolls

Method:

1 *Heat oil in a small pan, add onion and garlic and fry until onion is soft. Stir in curry paste and cook a little. Add lemon juice and stir to mix. Set aside. Combine the ground chicken, breadcrumbs, salt, pepper and coriander and add the onion/curry mixture. Mix well.*

2 *Place a thawed sheet of puff pastry on work surface and cut in half across the centre. Pile a $^1/_4$ of the ground chicken mixture in a thick $1^1/_2$cm/$^1/_2$in wide strip along the centre of the strip. Brush the exposed pastry at the back with water, lift the front strip of pastry over the filling and roll to rest onto the back strip. Press lightly to seal. Cut the roll into 4 or 5 equal portions. Repeat with second half and then with second sheet. Glaze with milk and sprinkle with sesame seeds. Place onto a flat baking tray.*

3 *Cook in a preheated hot oven 220°C/440°F/Gas 7 for 10 minutes, reduce heat to 180°C/350°F/Gas 4 and continue cooking for 15 minutes until golden brown. Serve hot as finger food.*
Tip: May be made in advance and reheated in a moderate oven. Yields 16-20

Serves 4

ingredients

2 teaspoons canola oil
1 medium onion, finely chopped
1 small clove garlic, crushed
2 teaspoons mild curry paste
1$^1/_2$ tablespoons lemon juice
500g/1 lb ground chicken
3 tablespoons dried breadcrumbs
$^1/_2$ teaspoon salt
$^1/_2$ teaspoon pepper
**2 tablespoons chopped
fresh coriander**
2 sheets frozen puff pastry with canola
1 tablespoon milk for glazing
1 tablespoon sesame seeds

chicken
cocktail balls in plum sauce

Method:

1 *In a food processor place all chicken ball ingredients except frying oil and process together quickly. With wetted hands shape into small balls. Place on a flat tray in a single layer and refrigerate for 30 minutes.*

2 *Heat oil, at least 5cm deep in a frying pan, or half full in a deep fryer, to 180°C/350°F. Deep fry for about 3 to 4 minutes. Remove and drain on absorbent paper. Place a cocktail stick in each ball and arrange on platter. Place dipping sauce in a bowl and serve with the chicken balls.*

Plum Sauce: *Place all ingredients in a small saucepan and bring slowly to the boil while stirring. Simmer for 2 minutes. Remove from heat and cool. Pour into a small bowl.*

Serves 4

ingredients

500g/1lb ground chicken
10 shallots, finely chopped
¼ teaspoon five spice powder
1½ tablespoons honey
1 teaspoon lemon zest
2 tablespoons lemon juice
1½ cups/90g/3oz fresh breadcrumbs
oil for frying

Plum Sauce
1 cup/250g/8oz plum jam
½ cup/125ml/4 fl oz white vinegar
¼ teaspoon ground ginger
¼ teaspoon ground allspice
⅛ teaspoon hot chilli powder

chicken
empanadas

Method:

1 *Sift the flour and salt into a bowl, add butter and rub in with fingertips until fine like breadcrumbs. Mix egg and sour cream together, add to flour mixture and mix to a dough. Wrap in plastic wrap and refrigerate 30 minutes.*

2 *Heat butter in a pan, add onions and sauté a few minutes. Add ground chicken meat and stir while cooking until ground chicken changes colour to white and then to a slightly golden colour. Stir in chopped peach, salt and pepper. Allow to cool.*

3 *Roll out dough between 2 sheets of greaseproof paper. Remove top sheet. Cut rounds of pastry about 10 to 12 cm in diameter. Place heaped teaspoon of filling in the centre of each round, moisten edges with water and fold over. Pinch edges well together or press with prongs of a fork. Glaze with milk and bake in a preheated oven 200°C/400°F/Gas 6 for 10 to 15 minutes. Serve hot or cold as fingerfood, a snack, or a meal with vegetable accompaniments.*

Makes 15-25

ingredients

Sour Cream Pastry
2¹/₂ cups/310g/10oz plain flour
pinch of salt
180g/6oz butter
1 egg
¹/₂ cup/125ml/4oz sour cream

Filling
1¹/₂ tablespoons butter or oil
1 onion, finely chopped
500g/1 lb ground chicken meat
1 cup/250g/8oz canned peach slices, finely chopped
salt, pepper

Oven temperature 200°C, 400°F, Gas 6

chicken
lemon balls

Method:

1 Place ground chicken meat in a bowl, grate onion into the ground chicken so as to catch juice also. Add egg, parsley, rice, salt and pepper to taste. Shape into balls the size of a walnut with wet hands. In a large saucepan heat butter and sauté onion until s o f t

Add water and stock cubes and bring to the boil. Drop the chicken balls into the boiling stock, reduce heat, cover and simmer for 40 minutes. Strain stock from chicken balls into a small saucepan keeping chicken balls covered and hot. Blend cornflour with 2 tablespoons cold water, add to the stock and stir until it boils and thickens, reduce heat and simmer.

2 Beat eggs and lemon juice together. Add spoonfuls of thickened stock to the egg mixture while beating the egg constantly. When half the stock is added return egg mixture to remaining sauce and stir for a little over very low heat.

Place chicken balls into serving dish and pour over the sauce. Garnish with parsley and lemon. Serve with crusty bread and a side salad.

Serves 4-6

ingredients
500g/1 lb ground chicken meat
1 onion, finely chopped
1 onion, finely grated
2 cups/500ml/16fl oz water
1 egg, beaten
2 chicken stock cubes
2 tablespoons chopped parsley
1 ½ tablespoons cornflour
¼ cup/55g/2oz raw rice
2 eggs
salt, pepper
3 tablespoons lemon juice
1 tablespoon butter

four
cheese calzone

Method:

1 Melt butter in a frying pan over a medium heat, add onion and cook for 3-4 minutes or until soft. Remove onion from pan and set aside. Add chicken to pan and cook for 3-4 minutes or until it changes colour.

2 Roll out pastry to 5mm/¼in thick and cut out a 30cm/12in round. Spread ricotta cheese over pastry round, leaving a 2cm/¾in border around the edge. Top one half of pastry with mozzarella cheese, onion, chicken, salami, artichokes and black pepper to taste. Combine tasty cheese (mature cheddar) and Parmesan cheese and sprinkle three-quarters of the mixture over filling.

3 Brush border of pastry round with egg mixture, fold uncovered side over filling, rolling edges to seal, then crimp or flute to make a neat and decorative border.

4 Place calzone on a lightly greased baking tray, brush with egg mixture, sprinkle with remaining cheese mixture and bake for 20-25 minutes or until puffed and golden. Stand for 5-10 minutes before serving.

Note: A calzone is basically a pizza folded over to encase the filling. Because the filling is sealed in during baking it is much more succulent. This easy variation only needs a tossed green salad to make a complete meal.

Serves 4

ingredients

30g/1oz butter
1 onion, sliced
250g/8oz lean ground chicken
375g/12oz prepared puff pastry
125g/4oz ricotta cheese, drained
125g/4oz mozzarella cheese, sliced
4 slices Italian salami, chopped
3 canned artichokes, drained and sliced
freshly ground black pepper
60g/2oz tasty cheese (mature cheddar), grated
45g/1½oz grated fresh Parmesan cheese
1 egg, lightly beaten with 1 tablespoon water

Oven temperature 220°C, 425°F, Gas 7

chicken
leek and potato pie

Method:

1 To make pastry, place cream cheese, tasty cheese (mature cheddar) and butter in a bowl and beat until soft and creamy. Mix in flour, sesame seeds and egg yolks to make a stiff dough. Turn dough onto a lightly floured surface and knead briefly. Wrap in plastic food wrap and refrigerate for 30 minutes.

2 To make filling, melt butter in a frying pan over a medium heat, add leeks and cook, stirring, for 3-4 minutes or until soft. Stir in chicken and cook for 4-5 minutes longer or until chicken changes colour. Stir in stock cube and black pepper to taste. Set aside to cool.

3 Roll out two-thirds of the pastry and use to line the base and sides of a 20cm/8in springform cake tin. Line with nonstick baking paper and fill with uncooked rice. Bake for 10 minutes, then remove rice and paper and bake for 10 minutes longer or until pastry is golden. Set aside to cool.

4 Spread half the chicken mixture over base of pastry shell, then top with half the potato slices. Repeat layers, finishing with a layer of potato. Combine cream, stock, egg and chives and pour over chicken.

5 Roll out remaining pastry large enough to cover pie. Brush rim of pastry shell with egg mixture and place pastry lid over filling, gently press edges together to seal then trim to neaten. Brush pie top with egg mixture. Make slits in top of pie using a small shape knife and bake for 15 minutes. Reduce temperature to 190°C/375°F/ Gas 5 and bake for 30 minutes.

Note: Great hot, warm or cold, this pie is a spectacular dish for a special picnic. When ground chicken is unavailable buy skinless, boneless chicken breast or thigh fillets and ground it yourself, alternatively you can use a whole chicken or chicken pieces, these will take a little more preparation as you will need to remove the skin and bones before grounding.

Serves 6

ingredients

1 egg, lightly beaten with 1 tablespoon water

Cheese pastry
60g/2oz cream cheese, softened
75g/2¹/₂oz tasty cheese (mature cheddar), grated
125g/4oz butter, softened
1¹/₂ cups/185g/6oz flour, sifted
3 tablespoons sesame seeds
2 egg yolks

Leek and chicken filling
60g/2oz butter
3 leeks, sliced
375g/12oz lean ground chicken meat
1 chicken stock cube
freshly ground black pepper
1 large potato, cooked and sliced
¹/₂ cup/125mL/4fl oz cream (double)
¹/₄ cup/60mL/2fl oz chicken stock
1 egg, lightly beaten
3 tablespoons snipped fresh chives

Oven temperature 220°C/425°F/Gas 7

herbed
chicken loaf

Photograph page 45

ingredients

750g/1 1/2 lb ground chicken meat
100g/3oz lean ham, diced
1/2 cup/30g/1oz green shallots, sliced finely
2 tablespoons fresh chopped herbs
(tarragon, thyme, parsley,
sage or dill are suitable)
2 slices wholemeal bread,
made into breadcrumbs
2 eggs, beaten
1 teaspoon salt
freshly ground pepper
3 tablespoons whisky (or use apple juice)

For sauce
1 cup/250ml/8fl oz natural yoghurt
1 tablespoon chopped herbs
1 teaspoon finely grated lemon rind

Method:
1 Line a loaf pan with baking paper.
2 Combine all ingredients. Press into loaf pan, cover with foil. Place in a larger pan with sufficient water to come halfway up sides of chicken loaf pan. Bake in a moderate oven for 50 minutes. (Or use a microsafe loaf pan and cook on medium for 15-18 minutes.) Whichever cooking method is used, allow to stand for 10 minutes before turning out.
3 To make sauce, combine yoghurt, herbs and lemon rind. Serve sliced with sauce, either hot or cold.
Serves 4-6

chicken
stuffed eggplant (aubergine)

ingredients

500g/1lb ground chicken meat
1 medium onion, chopped finely
2 tablespoons chopped parsley
1/2 teaspoon allspice
1/2 teaspoon cinnamon
1 tablespoon pine nuts
4 eggplants (aubergine),
about 175-200g/6-7oz each
1 cup/250g/8fl oz tomato purée
1/2 teaspoon salt
1/2 teaspoon sugar
1 tablespoon olive oil

Method:
1 Combine ground chicken meat, onion, parsley, spices and pine nuts.
2 Make 3 or 4 slashes in each eggplant (aubergine), taking care not to cut right through. Stuff chicken mixture into each slash. Place eggplants (aubergines) in a roaster pan, so that they fit snugly together. Pour tomato purée into dish. Sprinkle with salt and pepper. Drizzle over the olive oil and bake, uncovered, in a moderate oven for 40 minutes (or microwave on HIGH for 15-18 minutes). Serve hot, garnished with parsley, with salad and bread.
Serves 4

chicken
and rice balls

Method:

1 Cover rice with cold water and leave for 2 hours, drain well and place in a shallow dish.
2 Combine remaining ingredients and form into small balls.
3 Roll chicken balls in rice so that rice coats the entire surface.
4 Place rice balls in the top part of a bamboo or stainless steel steamer so that they are not touching each other. Steam with lid on for 15 minutes. Stand for 3-4 minutes. Serve with a small bowl of salt-reduced soy sauce for dipping. Not suitable to microwave.

Note: Batches of chicken and rice balls can be made in advance and stored in the refrigerator or freezer in plastic lock bags until required.

Makes 18

ingredients

1 cup/155g/5oz long grain rice
400g/13oz ground chicken meat
³/₄ cup/45g/1¹/₂oz finely chopped mushrooms
Small can water chestnuts,
drained and chopped finely
3 shallots, sliced finely
1 teaspoon finely chopped ginger
1 tablespoon soy sauce
2 egg whites

chicken
patties

Method:

1 Place ground chicken meat in a bowl, add remaining ingredients except oil. Mix well to distribute ingredients.
2 With wet hands shape into 4 or 5 flat patties.
3 Heat grill on high, line with foil, brush foil with oil. Cook about 5 minutes on each side. For pan fry heat a little oil in a heavy based frying pan, cook about 3 minutes on each side. Patties may also be cooked on a barbecue plate.

Serve hot with vegetable accompaniments.

Serves 4-5

ingredients

500g/1 lb ground chicken meat
1/2 cup/60g/2 oz dried breadcrumbs
1 clove garlic, crushed
1 teaspoon salt
1/4 teaspoon pepper
2 tablespoons lemon juice
1 egg
1/4 cup/60ml/2 fl oz water
a little oil for frying

Oven temperature 220°C, 440°F, Gas 7

chicken
pie supreme

ingredients

3 rashers bacon, diced
2 large onions, finely chopped
125g/4oz mushrooms, sliced
¹/₂ red capsicum (pepper), diced
500g/1 lb ground chicken
¹/₂ teaspoon mixed herbs
2 tablespoons lemon juice
salt, pepper to taste
1¹/₂ tablespoons flour
³/₄ cup/180ml/6fl oz milk
2 sheets frozen puff pastry

Method:

1 Heat a large wide based saucepan, add bacon and cook till fat runs. Add onion, mushrooms and capsicum (pepper), stir well, turn down heat to low, cover and allow to sweat for 3 minutes. Stir occasionally. Add ground chicken, increase heat and stir until meat becomes white, then slightly brown. Add herbs, lemon juice and seasonings. Sprinkle in flour and mix well, then gradually stir in milk. Heat until mixture thickens. Set aside to cool.

2 Grease a large flat oven tray lightly. Cut off a 7¹/₂cm/3in strip of pastry from one sheet and place large portion onto baking tray. Pile chicken mixture in a neat rectangle 2¹/₂cm/1in in from each edge. Brush border with water and place over second sheet, moulding it down the sides of the chicken and pressing around the border to seal. Trim edges cutting through both layers then make cuts at 1cm/¹/₂in intervals around base to flute the edges. Brush all over with egg and milk glaze and decorate with lattice strips cut from trimmings. Glaze lattice. Cut 2 slits in top of pie. Bake in a preheated oven 220°C/440°F/Gas 7 for 10 minutes, reduce heat to 190°C/370°F/Gas 5 and cook 25 minutes more.

Serve hot with vegetable accompaniments.

Serves 4

chicken
ball soup

Method:

1 *Place ground chicken into a bowl, add chilli powder, salt, pepper, egg and breadcrumbs. Mix thoroughly to combine ingredients. Refrigerate for 20 minutes.*

2 *In a large saucepan heat butter, add shallots and sauté until soft. Add chicken stock or water and stock cubes and bring to the boil.*

3 *With wet hands roll ground chicken into small balls. Drop into the boiling stock, reduce heat and simmer 10 minutes. Stir in the creamed corn and simmer 2 minutes to heat well. Garnish with shallot curl, serve with crusty bread.*

Serves 2-4

ingredients

250g/8oz ground chicken
¹/₄ teaspoon Mexican style chilli powder
¹/₂ teaspoon salt
¹/₄ teaspoon pepper
I egg
2 tablespoons stale bread crumbs
I tablespoon butter
8 shallots, chopped
4 cups/32oz chicken stock or
4 cups/32oz water and 3 stock cubes
440g/15oz can creamed style
sweet corn

spicy lamb rolls

ground lamb

Lamb was the first meat to grace

the table of mankind. Its popularity still ranks amongst the first preference, for it is a fine to medium grained meat with a velvety texture and a delightful sweetish flavour. Ground lamb has a pleasant taste and is tender and moist. It is not uncommon for cooks to mix a little ground lamb with ground beef to add more flavours to meat loaves and patties.

spicy
lamb rolls

Photograph page 51

Method:

1 *Heat oil in a frying pan over a medium heat, add onion and cook for 2-3 minutes or until soft.*

2 *Add lamb, tomato paste (purée), honey, cinnamon, allspice, mint, lemon juice and lemon rind to pan and cook, stirring, for 5 minutes or until meat is brown. Remove pan from heat and set to cool. Stir in pine nuts.*

3 *Layer 4 sheets of pastry, brushing each with melted butter. Cut pastry in half, lengthways, then cut each half into quarters. Place a spoonful of meat mixture on one edge of each pastry piece and roll up, tucking in sides to make a thin roll. Repeat with remaining pastry and filling.*

4 *Place rolls on a baking tray, brush with remaining butter and bake for 10-15 minutes or until pastry is golden and filling cooked.*

Note: *If you do not have a food processor, mix the ground meat and other ingredients together in a bowl. The texture will not be as fine but the result and taste will be just as good. For a finer texture purchase fine ground lamb or grind it again yourself before preparing the rolls.*

Serves 4

ingredients

1 tablespoon olive oil
1 onion, finely chopped
315g/10oz lean ground lamb
1 tablespoon tomato paste (purée)
2 teaspoons honey
$\frac{1}{4}$ teaspoon ground cinnamon
$\frac{1}{2}$ teaspoon ground allspice
2 teaspoons finely chopped fresh mint
2 teaspoons lemon juice
$\frac{1}{2}$ teaspoon finely grated lemon rind
1 tablespoon pine nuts
16 sheets filo pastry
125g/4oz butter, melted

Oven temperature 220°C, 425°F, Gas 7

greek
lamb kebabs

Method:

1 Combine lemon juice, olive, oil, garlic, lemon thyme and salt and pepper in a bowl, and marinate the lamb for at least 1-2 hours, or overnight (if time permits).

2 Combine all salad ingredients in a bowl and set aside.

3 Mix all the ingredients for the yoghurt sauce together in a bowl, and set aside.

4 Chargrill the lamb pieces for a few minutes each side until lamb is cooked (but still slightly pink). Fill each pita bread with the lamb, salad and yoghurt sauce, and serve warm.

Serves 4-6

ingredients

1/2 cup/60ml/2fl oz lemon juice
1/3 cup/80ml/3fl oz olive oil
1 clove garlic (crushed)
1 teaspoon lemon thyme (chopped)
salt/pepper
350g/12oz trim lamb (cubed)
4 pieces of small pita bread

Salad
1 Lebanese cucumber (cubed)
2 Roma tomatoes (quartered)
1 Spanish onion (sliced)
50g/2oz feta cheese (crumbled)
2 tablespoons olive oil
1 tablespoon vinegar
salt and pepper

Yoghurt Sauce
200g/7oz natural yoghurt
1 clove garlic (crushed)
100g/3oz cucumber (grated)
1 teaspoon mint (chopped)
salt and pepper to taste

moussaka
filled shells

Photograph page 55

Method:

1 Cut eggplant (aubergines) in half, lengthwise. Scoop out flesh leaving a 5mm/¹/₄in shell. Chop flesh and reserve to make the purée. Sprinkle eggplant (aubergine) shells with salt, turn upside down and set aside to stand for 20 minutes. Rinse shells under cold running water and pat dry. Brush eggplant (aubergine) shells inside and out with olive oil and place on a baking tray.

2 To make meat sauce, heat 1 tablespoon olive oil in a nonstick frying pan over a medium heat, add onion and garlic and cook, stirring, for 2-3 minutes or until onion is soft. Stir in lamb and cook until meat is brown. Add tomato supreme, wine, stock, basil, parsley and black pepper to taste to pan, or until mixture reduces and thickens.

3 To make cheese sauce, melt butter in a saucepan over a medium heat. Add flour and nutmeg and cook, stirring, for 3 minutes. Remove pan from heat and whisk in milk and sour cream. Return pan to heat and cook, stirring, for 3-4 minutes or until sauce boils and thickens. Remove pan from heat and stir in cheese.

4 Divide meat sauce between eggplant (aubergine) shells, top with cheese sauce, sprinkle with Parmesan cheese and dot with butter. Bake for 20-25 minutes or until filling is hot and bubbling and top is golden.

5 To make purée, place reserved eggplant (aubergine) flesh, ¹/₄ cup/60 mL/2 fl oz olive oil, garlic and onion in a nonstick frying pan and cook over a medium heat, stirring, for 4-5 minutes or until eggplant (aubergine) is soft. Place eggplant (aubergine) mixture, parsley, lemon juice and black pepper to taste in a food processor or blender and process until smooth. Serve with Moussaka-filled Shells.

Note: The tomato supreme used in this recipe consists of tomatoes, celery, peppers and various spices, if it is unavailable use canned tomatoes instead.

Serves 4

ingredients

2 large eggplant (aubergines)
salt
olive oil
45g/1¹/₂oz grated Parmesan cheese
30g/1oz butter

Meat sauce
1 onion, finely chopped
1 clove garlic, crushed
500g/1 lb lean lamb ground meat
315g/10oz canned tomato supreme
¹/₂ cup/125mL/4fl oz dry white wine
¹/₂ cup/125mL/4fl oz chicken stock
2 tablespoons finely chopped fresh basil
1 tablespoon finely chopped fresh parsley
freshly ground black pepper

Cheese sauce
60g/2oz butter
¹/₄ cup/30g/1oz flour
¹/₄ teaspoon ground nutmeg
1 cup/250mL/8fl oz milk
¹/₂ cup/125g/4oz sour cream
125g/4oz tasty cheese (mature cheddar), grated

Eggplant (Aubergine) purée
reserved eggplant (aubergine) flesh
1 clove garlic, crushed
1 small onion, grated
3 tablespoons chopped fresh parsley
2 tablespoons lemon juice

Oven temperature 180°C/350°F/Gas 4

mint glazed
lamb loaves

Method:

1   *Place lamb, cooked burghul (cracked wheat), mint, egg, stock cube and black pepper to taste in a food processor and process to combine. Divide mixture into four portions and press into rectangles each measuring 10x15cm/4x6in.*

2   *To make filling, place burghul (cracked wheat) in a bowl cover with boiling water and set aside to stand for 15 minutes. Drain and rinse under cold water. Squeeze burghul (cracked wheat) to remove excess water and place in a bowl. Add breadcrumbs, parsley, mint, lemon rind, pine nuts, mint jelly, apple, butter and black pepper to taste and mix to combine.*

3   *Divide filling between meat rectangles and spread to cover surface, leaving a 2cm/3/4in border. Roll up meat like a Swiss roll and pinch ends together to seal. Place rolls, seam side down in a lightly greased baking dish.*

4   *To make glaze, place mint jelly in a saucepan and heat for 3-4 minutes or until jelly melts. Stir in orange juice and maple syrup or honey and cook for 1-2 minutes longer. Brush rolls with glaze and bake, brushing with glaze several times, for 35-40 minutes or until cooked.*

Serves 4

ingredients

500g/1 lb lean lamb ground meat
**1/4 cup/45g/11/2oz burghul (cracked wheat),
cooked and drained**
1 tablespoon chopped fresh mint
1 egg, lightly beaten
1/2 chicken stock cube
freshly ground black pepper

Wheat and mint filling
1/3 cup/60g/2oz burghul (cracked wheat)
1/2 cup/30g/1oz fresh breadcrumbs
3 tablespoons finely chopped fresh parsley
1 tablespoon finely chopped fresh mint
1 teaspoon finely grated lemon rind
1 tablespoon pine nuts, toasted
2 teaspoons mint jelly
1 apple, cored, peeled and grated
15g/1/2oz butter, melted

Mint glaze
3 tablespoons mint jelly
2 tablespoons orange juice
1 tablespoon maple syrup or honey

Oven temperature 180°C/350°F/Gas 4

lamb sausages
in pitta pockets

Method:

1 Place lamb, sausage meat, onion, chopped garlic, mint, parsley, lemon rind, egg white and black pepper to taste in a bowl and mix to combine. Shape mixture into six thick sausages.

2 Cook sausages, turning frequently, on a lightly oiled preheated medium barbecue for 15-20 minutes or until cooked. Place cucumbers, crushed garlic, yoghurt, mint and black pepper to taste in a bowl and mix to combine.

3 Top each pitta bread oval with a sausage, then with a spoonful of yogurt mixture. Serve immediately.

Note: When shaping ground meat, dampen your hands and work on a lightly floured or dampened surface – this will prevent the ground meat from sticking to your hands and the surface.

Serves 6

ingredients

250g/8oz lean lamb ground meat
250g/8oz sausage meat
1 onion, finely chopped
2 cloves garlic, finely chopped
2 tablespoons finely chopped fresh mint
2 tablespoons finely chopped fresh parsley
2 teaspoons finely grated lemon rind
1 egg white, lightly beaten
freshly ground black pepper
2 small cucumbers, chopped
1 clove garlic, crushed
250g/8oz natural yoghurt
1 tablespoon finely chopped fresh mint
6 pitta bread ovals

lamb
ragout with vegetables

Photograph page 59

Method:

1 *To make ragoût, place lamb, breadcrumbs, garlic, spring onion, parsley and egg in a bowl and mix to combine. Shape mixture into small meatballs. Heat 1 tablespoon oil in a large saucepan and cook meatballs in batches for 3-4 minutes or until brown.*

2 *Heat remaining oil in same pan, add celery and onion and cook for 3-4 minutes or until onion is soft. Stir in flour and cook, stirring, for 1-2 minutes or until flour is brown. Remove pan from heat and gradually whisk in wine, stock and tomato purée. Return pan to heat and bring to the boil. Reduce heat, add lemon rind, thyme, beans and meatballs and simmer, uncovered, for 30 minutes.*

3 *Place couscous in a bowl, pour over 2 cups/500mL/16fl oz boiling water and toss with a fork until couscous absorbs almost all the liquid.*

4 *Boil, steam or microwave turnip, carrot, potato, cauliflower, parsnip, zucchini (courgette) and sweet potato until tender. To serve, arrange couscous around the edge of a large serving platter, pile vegetables in the centre, then top with ragoût.*

Note: *Often thought of as a type of grain couscous is actually a pasta made from durum wheat, however cook and use it in the same way as a grain. The name couscous refers to both the raw product and the cooked dish. It is an excellent source of thiamin and iron as well as being a good source of protein and niacin. Considered to be the national dish of Morocco, couscous is also used widely in the cuisines of Algeria and Tunisia.*

Serves 4

ingredients

1 cup/185g/6oz couscous
1 turnip, quartered
1 large carrot, quartered
1 large potato, quartered
1/2 head cauliflower, broken into large florets
1 large parsnip, quartered
1 large zucchini (courgette), quartered
1 sweet potato, quartered

Lamb ragout
500 g/1 lb lean ground lamb
3/4 cup/45g/11/2oz breadcrumbs, made from stale bread
3 cloves garlic, crushed
1 spring onion, finely chopped
2 tablespoons finely chopped fresh parsley
1 egg, lightly beaten
2 tablespoons olive oil
1 stalk celery, chopped
1 onion, chopped
1 tablespoon flour
3/4 cup/185mL/6fl oz dry white wine
1 cup/250mL/8 fl oz chicken stock
1/2 cup/125mL/4 fl oz tomato purée
2 teaspoons finely grated lemon rind
1 tablespoon finely chopped fresh thyme or 1 teaspoon dried thyme
315g/10oz canned butter beans, drained and rinsed

lamb
and kidney loaf

Photograph page 61

Method:

1 Soak kidneys in a bowl of salted water for 10 minutes. Drain, then pat dry with absorbent kitchen paper. Cut into slices, discarding core and set aside.

2 Arrange bay leaves in the base of a greased 11x21cm/4¹/₂x8¹/₂in loaf tin and line tin with 4 bacon rashers.

3 Melt butter in a frying pan over a medium heat, add onion and cook for 2-3 minutes or until soft. Add kidneys and cook for 2-3 minutes or until they just change colour. Stir in brandy, thyme and green peppercorns and cook, stirring, for 5 minutes or until brandy reduces by half. Set aside to cool.

4 Place lamb, breadcrumbs, stock cube, tomato paste (purée), egg and kidney mixture in a bowl and mix to combine. Spoon lamb mixture into prepared loaf tin, lay remaining bacon rashers on top and cover with aluminium foil. Place tin in a baking dish with enough boiling water to come halfway up the sides of the tin and bake for 45 minutes. Remove foil, drain off juices and bake for 45 minutes longer or until meatloaf is cooked.

5 To make sauce, place sugar and butter in a frying pan and cook over a medium heat, stirring, for 3-4 minutes or until sugar dissolves. Stir in wine, brandy, chicken stock and green peppercorns, bring to simmering and simmer for 5 minutes or until sauce reduces and thickens. Whisk in cream, bring back to simmering and simmer for 2-3 minutes longer. Serve with meatloaf.

Note: Meatloaves are great when feeding a crowd and most are just as good cold as they are hot. Next time you are having a party why not serve a selection of cold meatloaves. Make them the day before and chill overnight; prior to serving cut the meatloaves into slices and arrange on beds of lettuce on large serving platters. Accompany with a selection of salads, mustards, chutneys and relishes and some crusty bread for a meal that is sure to appeal to all age groups.

Serves 8

ingredients

3 lamb kidneys, trimmed of all visible fat
3 bay leaves
6 rashers bacon, rind removed
30g/1oz butter
1 onion, finely chopped
¹/₄ cup/60 mL/2fl oz brandy
1 tablespoon finely chopped fresh thyme or 1 teaspoon dried thyme
1 tablespoon green peppercorns in brine, drained
750g/1¹/₂ lb lean ground lamb
³/₄ cup/45g/1¹/₂oz breadcrumbs, made from stale bread
¹/₂ chicken stock cube
1 tablespoon tomato paste (purée)
1 egg, lightly beaten

Green peppercorn sauce
2 tablespoons brown sugar
30g/1oz butter
¹/₄ cup/60mL/2fl oz red wine
2 tablespoons brandy
1 cup/250mL/8fl oz chicken stock
2 teaspoons green peppercorns in brine, drained
¹/₂ cup/125mL/4fl oz cream (double)

Oven temperature 180°C, 350°F, Gas 4

lamb and kidney loaf

spring roll baskets

ground
pork

Lean ground pork is 85% fat free,

made from the shoulder or forequarter which is trimmed of fat before mincing. Ground pork is the foundation of many patés and erines; it is used in forcemeat stuffings, fillings for pies, wantons, made into patties, meat loaves and meatballs. Ground pork is available from your local butcher or supermarket. It is best when used fresh, within a few days.

spring
roll baskets

Photograph page 59

Method:

1 Heat vegetable oil in a large saucepan until a cube of bread dropped in browns in 50 seconds. Place 2 spring roll or wonton wrappers, diagonally, one on top of the other, so that the corners are not matching. Shape wrappers around the base of a small ladle, lower into hot oil and cook for 3-4 minutes. During cooking keep wrappers submerged in oil by pushing down with the ladle to form a basket shape. Drain on absorbent kitchen paper. Repeat with remaining wrappers to make four baskets.

2 To make filling, heat peanut (groundnut) oil in a frying pan, add ginger, chilli and spring onions and stir-fry for 1 minute. Add pork and stir-fry for 5 minutes or until meat is brown. Add prawns (shrimp), soy sauce, fish sauce, honey, lemon juice, bean sprouts, carrot and coriander and stir-fry for 4-5 minutes longer or until prawns (shrimp) change colour.

3 To serve, spoon filling into baskets and sprinkle with cashews.

Note: Wonton or spring roll wrappers are available frozen from Asian food shops and some supermarkets.

Serves 4

ingredients

vegetable oil for deep-frying
8 spring roll or wonton wrappers, each
12$\frac{1}{2}$cm/5in square
2 tablespoons unsalted cashews,
toasted and chopped

Pork and prawn filling
1 tablespoon peanut (groundnut) oil
2 teaspoons finely grated fresh ginger
1 small fresh red chilli, finely chopped
4 spring onions, finely chopped
250g/8oz lean ground pork
125g/4oz uncooked prawns, (shrimp)
shelled and deveined
1 tablespoon soy sauce
2 teaspoons fish sauce
2 teaspoons honey
2 teaspoons lemon juice
30g/1oz bean sprouts
1 small carrot, cut into thin strips
1 tablespoon finely chopped fresh
coriander

spiced apricot
pork balls

Method:

1 Soak the diced apricots in the brandy for 1 hour.

2 In a large bowl, combine the ground meat with the remaining ingredients except the oil. Knead well by hand for 2 minutes to distribute ingredients evenly, making a fine-textured mixture. Cover and refrigerate for 1 hour to allow the flavours to blend.

3 Take a heaped teaspoon of mixture and roll into a ball with wet hands. Flatten slightly and press the centre with your thumb to form a deep depression. Place 1/4 teaspoon of soaked apricots in the depression and remould into a ball, covering the apricot dice. Place on a flat tray and continue to roll the remainder. Cover with plastic wrap and refrigerate for 30 minutes (or more) before frying.

4 Heat enough oil to be 1cm deep in a large, heavy-based frying pan or an electric fry pan set at 180°C/350°F. Fry the meat balls in 2 or 3 batches, rolling them around the pan to cook all over and keep their shape. Drain on kitchen paper. Place on a heated serving platter with dipping sauce in the centre and toothpicks for serving.

Apricot Dipping Sauce: *Place diced apricots and water in a saucepan with any remaining brandy-soaked apricots. Bring to the boil, turn down heat and simmer for 15 minutes or until very soft. Stir in sugar, vinegar and teriyaki sauce, and simmer for 2 minutes. Purée in a blender or pass through a sieve. Stir in the fresh ginger juice, serve with the apricot meat balls.*

Makes 20-25

ingredients

³/₄ **cup/120g/4oz dried apricots**
2 tablespoons brandy
500g/1 lb prime ground pork
1 medium onion, very finely chopped
**1 slice white bread, crusts removed
and soaked in ¹/₄ cup/60mL/2fl oz water**
¹/₂ teaspoon ground cinnamon
Pinch of ground nutmeg
1 teaspoon salt
¹/₂ teaspoon pepper
1 egg
oil for frying

apricot dipping sauce
¹/₂ cup/95g/3oz diced dried apricots
1 cup/250ml/8fl oz water
2 teaspoons sugar
2 teaspoons balsamic vinegar
1 teaspoon teriyaki sauce
1 teaspoon fresh ginger juice

ham roulade
with mustard sour cream sauce

Method:

1 Lightly oil roulade or Swiss roll pan. Line with non-stick baking paper, edges extending 12cm/5in at each end

2 In a large bowl combine ham, egg yolks, flour, butter, herbs, seasoning and Madeira. Beat egg whites until stiff and fold into ham mixture. Spread mixture into pan, bake in oven, preheated to 190°C/370°F/ Gas 5 for 20 minutes.

3 Turn out onto two overlapping sheets of non-stick baking paper, peel off lining paper. Use the non-stick paper to help roll up into a roulade. Place in serving dish.

4 Mix the sour cream with Dijon mustard, tarragon and chopped dill. Serve roulade sliced, with sauce. Serve with fresh garden salad.

Serves 4-6

ingredients

500g/1lb ham, finely ground
1 tablespoon olive oil
6 eggs, separated
4 tablespoons plain flour
4 tablespoons butter, melted and cooled
¹/₂ teaspoon ground pepper
2 tablespoons chopped parsley
2 tablespoons dried tarragon leaves
4 tablespoons Madeira wine

Sauce
1 cup/250ml/8fl oz sour cream
1 tablespoon Dijon mustard
1 tablespoon dried tarragon leaves
1 tablespoon chopped dill

Oven temperature 190°C, 370°F, Gas 5

sweet potato
and pork crumble

Method:

1 Melt butter in a frying pan over a medium heat, stir in orange juice, honey, brown sugar and ginger and cook for 2-3 minutes or until mixture is syrupy. Add sweet potatoes and toss to coat. Set aside.

2 Heat oil in a clean frying pan over a medium heat, add garlic and cinnamon and cook for 1 minute. Add pork and cook, stirring, for 5 minutes. Stir in tomato purée and port or wine, bring to the boil, then reduce heat and cook for 8 minutes or until most of the liquid evaporates. Place half the sweet potatoes in the base of a greased shallow ovenproof dish, top with pork mixture, then remaining sweet potatoes.

3 To make crumble, combine breadcrumbs, rolled oats, brown sugar and cinnamon in a bowl. Rub in butter and stir in pecans. Sprinkle over meat mixture and bake for 40 minutes.

Note: For something different make this recipe using pumpkin instead of sweet potatoes. You will need 750g-1kg/1 1/2-2 lb pumpkin.

ingredients

30g/1oz butter
1/4 cup/60mL/2fl oz orange juice
1 tablespoon honey
1 tablespoon brown sugar
1 teaspoon finely grated fresh ginger
2 sweet potatoes, cooked and sliced
1 tablespoon vegetable oil
1 clove garlic, crushed
1 teaspoon ground cinnamon
250g/8oz lean ground pork
1/4 cup/60mL/2fl oz tomato purée
1 tablespoon port or red wine

Pecan crumble
1 cup/60g/2oz wholemeal breadcrumbs, made from stale bread
1/2 cup/45g/1 1/2oz rolled oats
1/2 cup/90g/3oz brown sugar
1 teaspoon ground cinnamon
60g/2oz butter
60g/2oz chopped pecans

Oven temperature 180°C, 350°F, Gas 4

hungarian
pork slice

Photograph page 69

Method:

1 *Boil or microwave cabbage leaves until tender. Drain, refresh under cold water and drain again. Line a greased, shallow ovenproof dish with some of the cabbage leaves. Set remaining leaves aside.*

2 *Heat oil in a frying pan, add onion and garlic and cook until onion is soft. Cool. Combine pork, rice, breadcrumbs, milk, marjoram, caraway seeds, paprika, eggs, black pepper to taste and onion mixture.*

3 *Spoon half the pork mixture into cabbage-lined dish, top with a layer of cabbage leaves and the remaining pork. Arrange bacon over top, cover and bake for 1 hour or until cooked. Drain off cooking juices and reserve.*

4 *To make sauce, melt butter in a saucepan over a low heat, add flour and cook, stirring, for 2-3 minutes. Remove pan from heat and whisk in stock and reserved cooking juices. Return pan to heat and cook, stirring constantly, for 3-4 minutes or until sauce boils and thickens. Remove pan from heat and whisk in sour cream and black pepper to taste. To serve, invert slice onto a serving plate, cut into wedges and accompany with sauce.*

Note: *This slice is delicious served hot, warm or cold. Cold it is perfect in packed lunches or as part of a picnic feast. If serving it cold you may prefer to accompany the slice with a tasty tomato sauce.*

Serves 4

ingredients

¹/₂ **large cabbage, leaves separated**
1 tablespoon vegetable oil
1 onion, chopped
2 cloves garlic, crushed
500 g/1 lb lean ground pork
¹/₃ **cup/75g/2¹/₂oz short grain rice, cooked**
³/₄ **cup/45g/1¹/₂oz breadcrumbs,**
made from stale bread
¹/₂ **cup/125mL/4fl oz milk**
¹/₂ **teaspoon dried marjoram**
¹/₄ **teaspoon caraway seeds**
1 tablespoon ground paprika
2 eggs, lightly beaten
freshly ground black pepper
4 rashers bacon, rind removed

Sour cream sauce
30g/1oz butter
1 tablespoon flour
¹/₂ **cup/125mL/4fl oz chicken stock**
¹/₂ **cup/125g/4oz sour cream**

Oven temperature 180°C/350°F/Gas 4

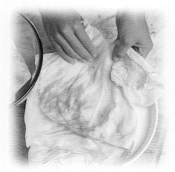  

chilli meat
pattie casserole

Photograph page 71

chilli meat pattie casserole

ingredients

500g/1 lb lean ground pork
2 tablespoons taco seasoning mix
1 egg
³/₄ cup/45g/1¹/₂oz breadcrumbs,
made from stale bread
250g/8oz tasty cheese (mature
cheddar), grated
vegetable oil
1 onion, finely chopped
1 small fresh red chilli, finely chopped
2 cloves garlic, crushed
440g/14oz canned tomatoes,
undrained and mashed
¹/₂ cup/125mL/4fl oz bottled
tomato salsa
1¹/₂ tablespoons tomato paste (purée)

<u>Hash brown topping</u>
2 large potatoes, scrubbed
2 eggs, lightly beaten
155g/5oz packet corn chips, crushed

Method:

1 *Place pork, taco seasoning mix, egg, breadcrumbs and half the cheese in a bowl and mix to combine. Shape meat mixture into eight patties.*

2 *Heat 2 tablespoons oil in a nonstick frying pan over a medium heat, add patties and cook for 3-4 minutes each side or until brown. Place patties in a shallow ovenproof dish and set aside.*

3 *Heat 1 tablespoon oil in pan over a medium heat, add onion, chilli and garlic and cook, stirring, for 3-4 minutes or until onion is soft. Stir in tomatoes, salsa and tomato paste (purée) and bring to the boil. Reduce heat and simmer for 5 minutes. Pour sauce over meat patties.*

4 *To make topping, boil, steam or microwave potatoes until just tender. Drain and refresh under cold running water. Peel potatoes and grate coarsely. Place potatoes, eggs and corn chips in a bowl and mix to combine.*

5 *Heat 2 tablespoons oil a large frying pan over a medium heat and cook spoonfuls of potato mixture for 3-4 minutes each side or until golden. Remove from pan, drain on absorbent kitchen paper and place slightly overlapping, on top of patties, sprinkle with remaining cheese and bake for 40 minutes.*

Serves 4

meatball
and noodle soup

Photograph page 73

meatball and noodle soup

ingredients

220g/7oz lean ground pork
125g/4oz lean ground chicken
I egg white, lightly beaten
4 tablespoons chopped fresh coriander
I teaspoon chilli paste (sambal oelek)
125g/4oz rice noodles
2 teaspoons vegetable oil
8 oyster mushrooms, stems removed
3 cups/750mL/I¹/₂pt chicken stock
I tablespoon lime juice
2 tablespoons fish sauce
I tablespoon brown sugar
I carrot, cut into thin strips
3 spring onions, cut into thin strips

<u>Oriental Dressing</u>
I teaspoon sesame oil
I teaspoon grated fresh ginger
2 teaspoons soy sauce
I tablespoon water
I teaspoon vinegar
¹/₄ teaspoon crushed garlic

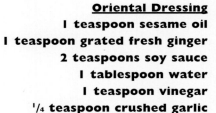

Method:

1 *Place pork, chicken, egg white, 2 tablespoons fresh coriander and chilli paste (sambal oelek) in a food processor and process to combine. Shape mixture into small balls and steam or microwave until cooked. Set aside.*

2 *Place noodles in a bowl, pour over boiling water to cover and set aside to stand for 8 minutes. Drain well. Heat oil in a large saucepan, add mushrooms and cook for 2 minutes. Stir in stock, lime juice, fish sauce and sugar, bring to the boil and boil for 5 minutes. Stir in carrot and*

spring onions and cook for I minute. Divide meatballs and noodles between soup bowls, ladle over hot soup and sprinkle with remaining coriander.

Note: *A tasty oriental-style soup that is a meal in itself. For a more substantial meal start or finish with naan bread and a salad of shredded chinese cabbage, chopped spring onions, chopped fresh basil and coriander tossed with oriental dressing. To make oriental dressing place ingredients in a screwtop jar and shake well to combine.*

Serves 4

pork
and apple cabbage rolls

Photograph page 75

Method:

1 *Heat oil in a frying pan over a medium heat, add onion and bacon and cook, stirring, for 3-4 minutes or until onion is soft. Stir in apple and caraway seeds and cook for 2 minutes longer. Remove pan from heat and set aside to cool.*

2 *Place pork, rice, egg, black pepper to taste and onion mixture in a bowl and mix to combine.*

3 *Boil, steam or microwave cabbage leaves until soft. Refresh under cold running water, pat dry with absorbent kitchen paper and trim stalks.*

4 *Divide meat mixture between cabbage leaves and roll up, tucking in sides. Secure with wooden toothpicks or cocktail sticks.*

5 *Melt 30g/1oz butter in a frying pan, add rolls and cook, turning several times, until lightly browned. Transfer rolls to a shallow ovenproof dish.*

6 *Melt remaining butter in pan over a medium heat, stir in paprika and flour and cook for 2 minutes. Stir in tomato paste (purée), wine and stock and bring to the boil. Reduce heat and simmer, stirring, for 5 minutes. Remove pan from heat and whisk in sour cream. Pour sauce over rolls, cover and bake for 1 hour.*

Note: *These rolls are delicious if made using ground lamb instead of the pork. This recipe is a good way to use up leftover cooked rice and spinach or silverbeet leaves can be used instead of cabbage.*

Serves 4

ingredients

2 tablespoons vegetable oil
1 onion, finely grated
2 rashers bacon, chopped
1 green apple, peeled, cored and grated
1 teaspoon caraway seeds
500g/1 lb lean ground pork
125g/4oz brown rice, cooked
1 egg, lightly beaten
freshly ground black pepper
8 large cabbage leaves
60g/2oz butter
1 ½ tablespoons paprika
1 ½ tablespoons flour
1 tablespoon tomato paste (purée)
½ cup/125mL/4fl oz red wine
1 ½ cups/375mL/12fl oz chicken stock
½ cup/125g/4oz sour cream

Oven temperature 180°C/350°F/Gas 4

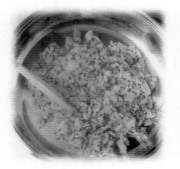

Method:

1 To make dough, place yeast and water in a bowl and whisk with a fork until yeast dissolves. Set aside in a warm draught-free place for 5 minutes or until foamy. Place butter and milk in a saucepan and cook over a medium heat, stirring constantly, until butter melts. Remove pan from heat and set aside until lukewarm. Pour milk mixture into yeast mixture, then stir in sugar, eggs and salt and beat to combine. Stir in flour and beat vigorously until mixture is smooth and satiny. Cover bowl with plastic food wrap and set aside in a warm draught-free place for 40 minutes or until doubled in volume.

2 To make filling, heat oil in a frying pan over a medium heat, add pork, garlic and ginger and cook, stirring, for 5 minutes or until meat is brown. Stir in hoisin sauce, oyster sauce, soy sauce, sesame oil and cornflour mixture and bring to the boil. Reduce heat and simmer for 5 minutes or until mixture thickens. Remove pan from heat, add spring onions and set aside to cool.

3 Turn dough onto a floured surface and knead for 10 minutes or until dough is smooth and no longer sticky. Roll dough out to 1cm/1/2in thick and using a 5cm/2in cutter, cut out twelve rounds.

4 Using your index finger make an indent in centre of half the dough rounds. Place a spoonful of filling in each indent. Brush remaining dough rounds with egg mixture and place over rounds with filling. Pinch edges together firmly and place buns on a greased baking tray, cover and set aside in a warm draught-free place for 30 minutes or until almost doubled in size. Bake for 10 minutes, then reduce temperature to 200°C/400°F/Gas 6 and bake for 5 minutes longer or until buns are golden.

5 To make glaze, place sugar and water in a saucepan and cook over a medium heat, stirring constantly, without boiling until sugar dissolves. Bring to boil, then boil rapidly until mixture becomes syrupy. Set aside to cool slightly. Brush warm buns with glaze.

sweet
pork buns

Photograph page 77

ingredients

30g/1oz fresh yeast, crumbled or
1 3/4 teaspoons active dry yeast
1/4 cup/60mL/2fl oz lukewarm water
60g/2oz butter
1 cup/250mL/8fl oz milk
1/4 cup/60g/2oz sugar
2 eggs, lightly beaten
1 teaspoon salt
3 3/4 cups/470g/15oz flour, sifted

Pork filling
2 teaspoons peanut (groundnut) oil
250g/8oz lean ground pork
1 clove garlic, crushed
1/2 teaspoon finely grated fresh ginger
1 tablespoon hoisin sauce
1 tablespoon oyster sauce
2 tablespoons soy sauce
1/2 teaspoon sesame oil
3 teaspoons cornflour blended with
1/2 cup/125mL/4fl oz chicken stock
3 spring onions, finely chopped
1 egg, lightly beaten with
1 tablespoon water

Glaze
1/4 cup/60g/2oz sugar
1/3 cup/90mL/3fl oz water

Note: There are two types of yeast commonly used in baking – fresh and dried. Dried yeast works as well as fresh but takes longer to activate. It is twice as concentrated as fresh yeast, so you will require half as much. You will find that 15g/1/2oz dried yeast has the same rising power as 30g/1oz fresh yeast. Fresh yeast is also known as baker's or compressed yeast.

Makes 6

Oven temperature 220°C/425°F/Gas 7

Cooking is not an exact science: one does not require finely calibrated scales, pipettes and scientific equipment to cook, yet the conversion to metric measures in some countries and its interpretations must have intimidated many a good cook.

Weights are given in the recipes only for ingredients such as meats, fish, poultry and some vegetables. Though a few grams/ounces one way or another will not affect the success of your dish.

Though recipes have been tested using the Australian Standard 250mL cup, 20mL tablespoon and 5mL teaspoon, they will work just as well with the US and Canadian 8fl oz cup, or the UK 300mL cup. We have used graduated cup measures in preference to tablespoon measures so that proportions are always the same. Where tablespoon measures have been given, these are not crucial measures, so using the smaller tablespoon of the US or UK will not affect the recipe's success. At least we all agree on the teaspoon size.

For breads, cakes and pastries, the only area which might cause concern is where eggs are used, as proportions will then vary. If working with a 250mL or 300mL cup, use large eggs (60g/2oz), adding a little more liquid to the recipe for 300mL cup measures if it seems necessary. Use the medium-sized eggs (55g/1^1/4oz) with 8fl oz cup measure. A graduated set of measuring cups and spoons is recommended, the cups in particular for measuring dry ingredients. Remember to level such ingredients to ensure their accuracy.

English measures

All measurements are similar to Australian with two exceptions: the English cup measures 300mL/10fl oz, whereas the Australian cup measure 250mL/8fl oz. The English tablespoon (the Australian dessertspoon) measures 14.8mL/^{1}/2fl oz against the Australian tablespoon of 20mL/^{3}/4fl oz.

American measures

The American reputed pint is 16fl oz, a quart is equal to 32fl oz and the American gallon, 128fl oz. The Imperial measurement is 20fl oz to the pint, 40fl oz a quart and 160fl oz one gallon.

The American tablespoon is equal to 14.8mL/^{1}/2fl oz, the teaspoon is 5mL/^{1}/6fl oz. The cup measure is 250mL/8fl oz, the same as Australia.

Dry measures

All the measures are level, so when you have filled a cup or spoon, level it off with the edge of a knife. The scale below is the "cook's equivalent"; it is not an exact conversion of metric to imperial measurement. To calculate the exact metric equivalent yourself, use 2.2046 lb = 1kg or 1 lb = 0.45359kg

Metric		Imperial	
g = grams		oz = ounces	
kg = kilograms		lb = pound	
15g		^{1}/2oz	
20g		^{2}/3oz	
30g		1oz	
60g		2oz	
90g		3oz	
125g		4oz	^{1}/4 lb
155g		5oz	
185g		6oz	
220g		7oz	
250g		8oz	^{1}/2 lb
280g		9oz	
315g		10oz	
345g		11oz	
375g		12oz	^{3}/4 lb
410g		13oz	
440g		14oz	
470g		15oz	
1,000g	1kg	35.2oz	2.2 lb
	1.5kg		3.3 lb

Oven temperatures

The Celsius temperatures given here are not exact; they have been rounded off and are given as a guide only. Follow the manufacturer's temperature guide, relating it to oven description given in the recipe. Remember gas ovens are hottest at the top, electric ovens at the bottom and convection-fan forced ovens are usually even throughout. We included Regulo numbers for gas cookers which may assist. To convert °C to °F multiply °C by 9 and divide by 5 then add 32.

Oven temperatures

	C°	F°	Regulo
Very slow	120	250	1
Slow	150	300	2
Moderately slow	150	325	3
Moderate	180	350	4
Moderately hot	190-200	370-400	5-6
Hot	210-220	410-440	6-7
Very hot	230	450	8
Super hot	250-290	475-500	9-10

Cake dish sizes

Metric	Imperial
15cm	6in
18cm	7in
20cm	8in
23cm	9in

Loaf dish sizes

Metric	Imperial
23x12cm	9x5in
25x8cm	10x3in
28x18cm	11x7in

Liquid measures

Metric	Imperial	Cup & Spoon
mL	fl oz	
millilitres	fluid ounce	
5mL	1/6fl oz	1 teaspoon
20mL	2/3fl oz	1 tablespoon
30mL	1fl oz	1 tablespoon plus 2 teaspoons
60mL	2fl oz	1/4 cup
85mL	2 1/2fl oz	1/3 cup
100mL	3fl oz	3/8 cup
125mL	4fl oz	1/2 cup
150mL	5fl oz	1/4 pint, 1 gill
250mL	8fl oz	1 cup
300mL	10fl oz	1/2 pint)
360mL	12fl oz	1 1/2 cups
420mL	14fl oz	1 3/4 cups
500mL	16fl oz	2 cups
600mL	20fl oz 1 pint,	2 1/2 cups
1 litre	35fl oz 1 3/4 pints,	4 cups

Cup measurements

One cup is equal to the following weights.

	Metric	Imperial
Almonds, flaked	90g	3oz
Almonds, slivered, ground	125g	4oz
Almonds, kernel	155g	5oz
Apples, dried, chopped	125g	4oz
Apricots, dried, chopped	190g	6oz
Breadcrumbs, packet	125g	4oz

	Metric	Imperial
Breadcrumbs, soft	60g	2oz
Cheese, grated	125g	4oz
Choc bits	155g	5oz
Coconut, desiccated	90g	3oz
Cornflakes	30g	1oz
Currants	155g	5oz
Flour	125g	4oz
Fruit, dried (mixed, sultanas etc)	185g	6oz
Ginger, crystallised, glace	250g	8oz
Honey, treacle, golden syrup	315g	10oz
Mixed peel	220g	7oz
Nuts, chopped	125g	4oz
Prunes, chopped	220g	7oz
Rice, cooked	155g	5oz
Rice, uncooked	220g	7oz
Rolled oats	90g	3oz
Sesame seeds	125g	4oz
Shortening (butter, margarine)	250g	8oz
Sugar, brown	155g	5oz
Sugar, granulated or caster	250g	8oz
Sugar, sifted icing	155g	5oz
Wheatgerm	60g	2oz

Length

Some of us still have trouble converting imperial length to metric. In this scale, measures have been rounded off to the easiest-to-use and most acceptable figures.

To obtain the exact metric equivalent in converting inches to centimetres, multiply inches by 2.54 whereby 1 inch equals 25.4 millimetres and 1 millimetre equals 0.03937 inches.

Metric	Imperial
mm=millimetres	in = inches
cm=centimetres	ft = feet
5mm, 0.5cm	1/4in
10mm, 1.0cm	1/2in
20mm, 2.0cm	3/4in
2.5cm	1in
5cm	2in
8cm	3in
10cm	4in
12cm	5in
15cm	6in
18cm	7in
20cm	8in
23cm	9in
25cm	10in
28cm	11in
30cm	1 ft, 12in

index

Recipe	Page	Recipe	Page
Beefy Egg Pies	23	**Ground Beef**	**8**
Burritos with Avocado Mayonnaise	20	**Ground Chicken**	**32**
Carpetburgers with Caper		**Ground Lamb**	**50**
Mayonnaise	10	**Ground Pork**	**62**
Chicken and Rice Balls	46	Ham Roulade with Mustard	
Chicken Apricot Roulade	34	Sour Cream Sauce	66
Chicken Ball Soup	49	Herbed Chicken Loaf	44
Chicken Cannelloni	35	Hungarian Pork Slice	68
Chicken Cocktail Balls		Lamb and Kidney Loaf	60
in Plum Sauce	37	Lamb Ragout with Vegetables	58
Chicken Empanadas	38	Lamb Sausages in Pitta Pockets	57
Chicken Leek and Potato Pie	43	Meatball and Bean Salad	28
Chicken Lemon Balls	41	Meatball and Noodle Soup	72
Chicken Patties	47	Middle Eastern Meatballs	15
Chicken Patties on Basil Flapjacks	39	Mint Glazed Lamb Loaves	56
Chicken Pie Supreme	48	Moussaka Filled Shells	54
Chicken Stuffed Eggplant		Nasi Goreng	12
(Aubergine)	44	New Spaghetti and Meatballs	22
Chilli Con Carne	11	**Points for Success**	**6**
Chilli Meat Pattie Casserole	70	Pork and Apple Cabbage Rolls	74
Clapshot pie	30	Sausage and Roasted Capsicum	
Classic Lasagne	29	(Pepper) Salad	14
Crispy Chilli Turnovers	19	Spiced Apricot Pork Balls	65
Crunchy Cottage Pie	16	Spicy Egg Balls	24
Curried Chicken Rolls	36	Spicy Lamb Rolls	52
Devilled Corn Muffins	18	Spring Roll Baskets	64
Four Cheese Calzone	42	Sweet Pork Buns	76
Greek Lamb Kebabs	53	Sweet Potato and Pork Crumble	67
Greek Style Chicken Rissoles		Wellington Bread Loaf	26
in Tomato Sauce	40		